INSIDE THE NBA

DALLAS MAVERICKS

BY DREW SILVERMAN

SportsZone

An Imprint of Abdo Publishing
abdobooks.com

abdobooks.com

Published by Abdo Publishing, a division of ABDO, PO Box 398166, Minneapolis, Minnesota 55439. Copyright © 2023 by Abdo Consulting Group, Inc. International copyrights reserved in all countries. No part of this book may be reproduced in any form without written permission from the publisher. SportsZone™ is a trademark and logo of Abdo Publishing.

Printed in the United States of America, North Mankato, Minnesota.
052022
092022

Cover Photo: Richard Rodriguez/Getty Images Sport/Getty Images
Interior Photos: Melinda Nagy/Shutterstock Images, 1; David J. Phillip/AP Images, 4, 9; Jeff Haynes/AFP/Getty Images, 6; Ronald Martinez/Getty Images Sport/Getty Images, 8, 18, 30; Mark Ralston/AFP/Getty Images, 11, 39; Focus on Sport/Getty Images Sport/Getty Images, 12, 16, 24, 27, 28, 34; Steven Dunn/Getty Images Sport/Getty Images, 15; Omar Vega/Getty Images Sport/Getty Images, 21; Christian Petersen/Getty Images Sport/Getty Images, 23; Don Emmert/Pool/Getty Images Sport/Getty Images, 32; Jonathan Bachman/ Getty Images Sport/Getty Images, 33; Eric Gay/AP Images, 37; Kevin C. Cox/Pool Getty Images/AP Images, 41

Editor: Charlie Beattie
Series Designer: Joshua Olson

Library of Congress Control Number: 2021951659

Publisher's Cataloging-in-Publication Data

Names: Silverman, Drew, author.
Title: Dallas Mavericks / by Drew Silverman
Description: Minneapolis, Minnesota: Abdo Publishing, 2023 | Series: Inside the NBA | Includes online resources and index.
Identifiers: ISBN 9781532198243 (lib. bdg.) | ISBN 9781098271893 (ebook)
Subjects: LCSH: Dallas Mavericks (Basketball team)--Juvenile literature. | Basketball--Juvenile literature. | Professional sports--Juvenile literature. | Sports franchises--Juvenile literature.
Classification: DDC 796.32364--dc23

TABLE OF
CONTENTS

CHAPTER ONE

BACKS AGAINST THE WALL

The Dallas Mavericks had their backs against the wall in Game 2 of the 2011 National Basketball Association (NBA) Finals. They were already down 1–0 after a 92–84 loss to the Miami Heat in Game 1. Now, with just over seven minutes remaining in Game 2, the Heat led by double digits.

With 7:14 left, Miami star guard Dwyane Wade gave his team an 88–73 advantage on a three-pointer from the corner. After Wade released his shot, he posed with his right arm extended in the air. The home crowd in Miami went wild as the ball dropped in.

Wade's shot capped a 13–0 Miami run. The Mavericks were sinking fast. They had never won the NBA championship. Their only other visit to the Finals was in 2006 against the same Miami Heat. Wade had torched them in a six-game Heat victory. It was starting to look like it would happen again.

Dirk Nowitzki was at the top of his game against the Miami Heat in the 2011 NBA Finals.

Nowitzki and the Mavericks were looking to avenge a disappointing 2006 NBA Finals loss to the Heat during the 2011 rematch.

SETTING THE STAGE

The 2010–11 Heat were one of the most star-studded teams in NBA history. Wade had been in Miami for seven years. But before the season, two of the NBA's best players signed up to join him. Center Chris Bosh came over in a trade from the Toronto Raptors. Forward LeBron James, one of the best players of his generation, left the Cleveland Cavaliers to sign with the Heat. James, Bosh, and Wade were all in their primes.

Dallas, on the other hand, had a roster full of aging stars. Sharp-shooting forward Dirk Nowitzki was the greatest player in Mavericks history. But he was 32 years old. Forward Shawn Marion was also 32, and guard Jason Terry was 33. Point guard Jason Kidd, once among the league's top players, was 38.

The Mavericks had made the playoffs for 11 consecutive seasons. However, they were running out of opportunities to win the title. They certainly did not want to fall behind 2–0 in the series against Miami's talented roster. Since 1978, only one team had lost the NBA Finals after winning the first two games. Oddly, that team was the Mavericks. They had been up 2–0 in 2006 before Miami came back to win four straight games.

A COMEBACK FOR THE AGES

When Wade's three-pointer swished through the net, the game appeared over. But the Maverick veterans disagreed.

Terry got Dallas going again by scoring six quick points. Marion added a driving layup. Kidd sank a three-pointer with just under four minutes left. When Terry added another basket at the 3:11 mark, Miami's lead was down to 90–86.

The Mavericks suddenly had momentum. Miami called a timeout, but it didn't help. The Heat turned the ball over right away. At the other end of the court, Terry drew two defenders. He made a bounce pass to Nowitzki, who drained a jump shot from the left wing.

It took nearly two minutes for anyone to score again. But the resilient Mavericks finally tied the game with 57.6 seconds

Dallas guard Jason Terry's hot shooting helped kickstart the Mavericks' comeback late in Game 2.

left. Nowitzki took a pass from Marion on a fast break and converted a left-handed layup to even the score at 90–90.

Dallas's run wasn't finished yet. After Wade missed at the other end, Nowitzki got open behind a screen from Dallas center Tyson Chandler. The German superstar knocked down a go-ahead three-pointer with 26.7 seconds remaining.

"A 20–2 run!" exclaimed television broadcaster Mike Breen. "One of the most incredible comebacks in NBA Finals history!"

NOT DONE YET

Despite Nowitzki's clutch shot, the Heat still had a chance. They took a timeout to move the inbounds pass to the frontcourt. As players slashed to get open, Dallas lost track of Miami guard Mario Chalmers. He faded to the far corner of the court. James whipped him a pass for a wide-open three-pointer. The game was tied again. Dallas's lead lasted only 2.2 seconds.

Still, the Mavericks had a chance to win. Once again, they went to Nowitzki. The forward used a hesitation dribble to beat Bosh, his primary defender. Miami forward Udonis Haslem raced from the far side of the court to help. But Nowitzki beat him to the basket and laid the ball in with his left hand with 3.6 seconds left on the clock.

James pushed the ball up the court in the final seconds. He passed to Wade, who attempted a long three-pointer on the run. When Wade's shot bounced off the rim at

Nowitzki goes up for the tiebreaking layup in the final seconds of Dallas's victory over the Heat in Game 2.

Award Winner

Nowitzki walked away with the Most Valuable Player (MVP) Award after the 2011 Finals. He led the Mavericks by averaging 26.0 points per game. He was also the leading rebounder on either team in the series, with 9.7 per game. Nowitzki was just the second European player ever to be named series MVP. Point guard Tony Parker of the San Antonio Spurs was the first, in 2007.

the buzzer, Nowitzki raised his right arm in the air. It was now his turn to celebrate. Nowitzki's teammates rushed onto the court to congratulate him.

Nowitzki had begun the night making just three of his first 11 shots. He ended it by making seven of his final 11. Most importantly, Dallas had won a critical game to tie the series at 1–1. The Mavericks had scored 22 of the final 27 points to steal the victory. Halfway through the fourth quarter, the team looked doomed. Now they had one of the best wins in team history.

"Definitely a huge comeback for us," said Nowitzki. "We never gave up."

Fueled by their Game 2 comeback, the Mavericks went on to win the NBA Finals in six games. With their backs against the wall, Nowitzki and the Mavs kept fighting on their way to a historic title.

Nowitzki holds up the trophy after Dallas defeated the Heat in six games to capture the Mavericks' first NBA title.

CHAPTER TWO

FOUR DECADES IN DALLAS

The Dallas Mavericks joined the NBA in 1980 as the league's twenty-third team. They got off to a rocky start. Dallas expected to find its first star in the 1980 NBA Draft. The team selected forward Kiki VanDeWeghe from the University of California, Los Angeles (UCLA) with the eleventh overall pick. There was only one problem. VanDeWeghe did not want to come to Dallas. He sat out and demanded a trade. VanDeWeghe eventually got his wish. The Mavericks sent him to the Denver Nuggets in December 1980. For the rest of his career, VanDeWeghe was booed whenever he played in Dallas.

It was an embarrassing first step. But the trade worked out for the Mavericks. They picked up Denver's first-round pick in the 1981 draft, which was ninth overall. Dallas also finished its first season with only 15 wins. At the time, a coin flip between the worst teams in each conference was used to decide the

Guard Rolando Blackman played the first 11 seasons of his NBA career in Dallas after being drafted in the first round in 1981.

top pick. Dallas won the toss over the Detroit Pistons. The Mavericks used the first pick on forward Mark Aguirre. They drafted guard Rolando Blackman ninth. Dallas also used its second-round pick on forward Jay Vincent. In one day, the Mavericks had picked up the core of an exciting young team.

GUNNING FOR THE POSTSEASON

It did not take long for the trio to lead Dallas into the postseason. In 1983–84 the Mavericks posted their first winning record of 43–39. They also won their first playoff series, knocking off the Seattle SuperSonics in five games. It was the start of five straight playoff appearances for the team.

Dallas reached new heights in 1986–87. The team won its first division title. Aguirre was one of the league's top scorers. The next season the Mavericks reached the Western Conference finals. There they faced the defending league champion Los Angeles Lakers. Dallas pushed the series to seven games before falling.

"I feel extremely proud . . . to be able to have been a part of this Maverick basketball team

New Kids in Town

The Mavericks were popular in Dallas from the very beginning. In 1980–81 the team set an NBA record for attendance by an expansion team. More than 319,000 fans came to Reunion Arena to see the Mavericks play that first season.

Small forward Mark Aguirre goes up for a dunk against the Los Angeles Lakers in the 1988 Western Conference finals.

that put this franchise on the map as being a great, great team," said Blackman.

It looked like the start of a great run for an exciting team. But the Mavericks fell apart quickly. Injuries took the roster apart over the next few seasons. Dallas made the playoffs again in 1989–90 but lost in the first round.

Forward Jamal Mashburn (32) was named to the NBA's All-Rookie team in 1993–94 after averaging 19.2 points per game.

SCUFFLING THROUGH THE NINETIES

Dallas's first stars were aging by the time the new decade started. Aguirre had been traded late in the 1988–89 season. Blackman was an All-Star the following year, but he was also 30 years old.

The Mavericks fell down the standings quickly. By 1992–93 they were 11–71. It was the second-worst NBA record in history at the time. The next year they started 1–20. The team also lost 20 consecutive games at one point. Dallas finished that year with only 13 wins.

The losing seasons meant high draft picks. The Mavericks selected fourth overall in 1992 and 1993. The first year they added guard Jim Jackson. In 1993 the pick was used on forward Jamal Mashburn. After another bad season, the Mavericks picked point guard Jason Kidd second overall.

The trio earned the nickname "the Three J's." All three were exciting young stars. Dallas won 36 games in 1994–95 with them playing together. But the Mavericks never improved. The next year Mashburn suffered a season-ending knee injury. Jackson and Kidd had trouble getting along. Kidd was an All-Star, but the team fell back to 26–56.

BUILDING A CONTENDER

Big changes came to the team the following year. Don Carter, who had owned the Mavericks since 1980, sold the team to H. Ross Perot Jr. Veteran coach Don Nelson was hired as the new general manager, and he tore apart the roster. The 1996–97 Mavericks used an NBA-record 27 players during the season. Only one player, rookie forward Samaki Walker, was on the team the entire year. By the end of the season, Nelson had traded all three of the J's—Jackson, Kidd, and Mashburn.

Coach Avery Johnson shouts instructions from the sidelines during the 2005 NBA playoffs.

Eventually, Nelson's moves paid off for Dallas. But it took time. The Mavericks took steps forward in 1997–98. Nelson took over as head coach early in the season. Then he made some key moves at the 1998 NBA Draft. First, he traded for point guard Steve Nash, who was struggling with the Phoenix Suns. Then, Nelson made a deal with the Milwaukee Bucks to swap first-round draft picks. The Mavericks picked up Dirk Nowitzki, a tall, skinny forward from Germany. Not many knew it at the time, but the trades would change Dallas forever.

Nash and Nowitzki combined with forward Michael Finley to lead Dallas back to the playoffs in 2000–01. By then the team had a new owner, tech billionaire Mark Cuban. The team played a fast-break style that kept fans entertained. A year later Dallas moved to a new arena. American Airlines Center was filled every night. After a decade of failure, the Mavericks were on the way back up.

It was not always a smooth road. Winning in the playoffs was tricky. Dallas reached the Western Conference finals in 2003. But a Nowitzki injury knocked him out of the final three games against the San Antonio Spurs. The Mavericks lost the series.

By the time Dallas won another playoff series, in 2005, two things had changed. Nash had left the team before the season as a free agent. Nelson was also gone. He had stepped down with 18 games left in the regular season. His replacement was former NBA point guard Avery Johnson.

Johnson's style was completely different. He stressed defense, and the Mavericks tightened up. It paid off in 2005–06, as Dallas finally reached the NBA Finals. After the team won the first two games over the Miami Heat, the city started planning a victory parade. That idea looked even better when the team held a 13-point lead with under seven minutes left in Game 3. But Dallas collapsed and lost the game. The Mavericks never recovered. The Heat won the next three games to take the championship.

MVP, MVP!

During Dirk Nowitzki's MVP season in 2006–07, he joined the exclusive 50–40–90 club of players who shoot at least 50 percent from the field, 40 percent from three-point range, and 90 percent from the foul line. At the time, Nowitzki was just the fifth player in league history to have a 50–40–90 season.

DALLAS DELIGHT

Dallas's playoff reputation took another hit the next year. The Mavericks finished 67–15 during the regular season. That was the best record in the NBA. But they melted down in a first-round loss to the Golden State Warriors. When the team lost in the first round again in 2008, Johnson was let go as head coach.

The Mavericks suffered two more early playoff exits under new head coach Rick Carlisle. But the team finally broke through in 2011. With Jason Kidd back on the roster, Dallas lost only three games in the first three playoff rounds. It once again faced off against the Miami Heat in the Finals. This time, Dallas lost Game 1. The Mavericks then rallied from a 15-point fourth-quarter deficit in Game 2. After Miami won Game 3, Dallas took over. Led by Nowitzki's MVP performance, the Mavericks won the next three games. They were champions for the first time.

"This is a special group," Nowitzki said after Dallas clinched the title. "We're world champions. That sounds unbelievable!"

Dallas won its championship with a veteran team. It could not sustain the success as the roster aged even more.

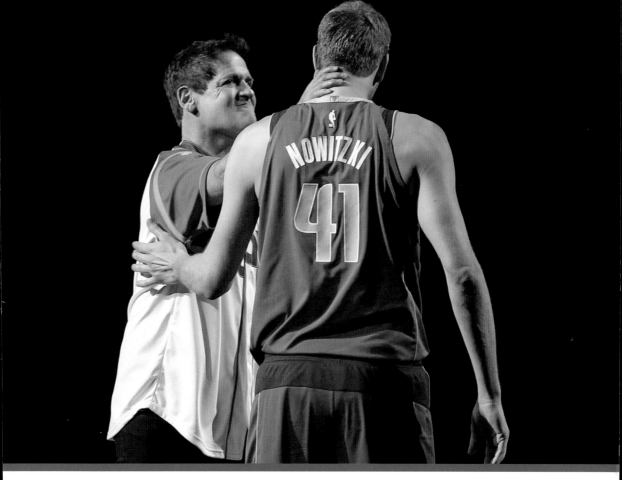

Mavericks owner Mark Cuban embraces Dirk Nowitzki during a ceremony that followed the legendary forward's final home game on April 9, 2019.

The Mavericks reached the postseason four of the next five seasons. But they never made it out of the first round.

In 2016–17 the Mavericks had a losing season for the first time since 1999–2000. Two more losing seasons followed. At the end of 2018–19, Nowitzki retired. He had spent 21 years with the team.

NEW SHERIFF IN TOWN

Dallas needed a new star. Luckily, the team already had one on its roster. At the 2018 NBA Draft, the Mavericks had the fifth pick. They had taken guard Trae Young but immediately traded him to the Atlanta Hawks. Coming back the other way was the third pick, guard Luka Dončić. The 6-foot-7-inch Slovenian was an immediate hit. He made the All-Rookie team his first season and led Dallas back to the playoffs in his second year.

As Dončić continued to improve, so did the Mavericks. In 2021–22 Dallas posted 52 wins, its most since the title-winning season of 2010–11.

Dončić missed the first three playoff games with a leg injury. But then he returned to lead Dallas to its first playoff series victory in a decade. And he didn't stop there. Dončić was brilliant in the second round against the top-seeded Phoenix Suns. He averaged 32.6 points, 9.9 rebounds, 7.0 assists, and 2.1 steals in the series. The All-Star capped his performance with back-to-back 30-point outings as the Mavericks rallied to win in seven games.

Their run finally ended in the conference finals against the powerhouse Golden State Warriors. But Dončić and the Mavericks had delivered a powerful statement to the league. Dallas was a contender again.

Luka Dončić, *right*, made his first All-NBA team after the 2019–20 season.

CHAPTER THREE

THE MIGHTIEST MAVS

Guard Brad Davis was ready to give up basketball in 1980. He had already been let go by three NBA teams. Now he was playing for a minor league team in Anchorage, Alaska. He just wanted to make enough money to finish school at the University of Maryland.

When the expansion Mavericks called asking if he wanted to sign, Davis said no. But assistant coach Bob Weiss convinced him to change his mind. Davis signed with the team in December. He promised to stay at least until the second college semester started in mid-January. If he didn't like it, he could take his NBA money and pay for school.

Fast forward to November 14, 1992. Davis was the first Dallas Maverick to have his number retired. His one-month stay stretched for 12 seasons and 883 regular-season games. Along

Dallas guard Brad Davis averaged a career-high 7.2 assists per game during the 1982–83 season.

the way Davis became a fan favorite for his hustle and passing skills. He had a team-record 4,524 assists when he retired.

THE CLASS OF 1981

Dallas's next stars came by a more traditional route. Dallas had two of the first nine picks in the 1981 draft. With the top overall selection, the Mavericks grabbed forward Mark Aguirre. Guard Rolando Blackman was the ninth pick.

The two players formed the backbone of the team for nearly a decade. As the Mavericks climbed up the standings, Aguirre and Blackman did most of the scoring. Until Dirk Nowitzki came along two decades later, the pair were the leading scorers in team history.

However, neither Aguirre nor Blackman led the team in scoring as a rookie. Second-round pick Jay Vincent averaged 21.4 points per game in 1981–82. The three young stars led Dallas to its first playoff appearance in 1984.

Davis, Aguirre, and Blackman were still with the team when Dallas reached the Western Conference finals in 1988. Aguirre finished as one of the top scorers in the NBA that season. Blackman was still a star. Derek Harper had taken over the starting point guard role for the veteran Davis. Harper joined the team in 1983–84 and improved every year. He stayed with the Mavericks until he was traded during the 1993–94 season.

Second-round pick Jay Vincent averaged 16.9 points and 6.5 rebounds per game during his five seasons in Dallas.

Then he came back again for one year in 1996–97. When he finally left the team, he had broken Davis's team assist record.

THE THREE J'S

Jim Jackson, Jamal Mashburn, and Jason Kidd all joined the team between 1992 and 1994. The three young stars looked as if they might bring Dallas back from a miserable start to the 1990s. In their first year together in 1994–95, the team

Point guard Jason Kidd left the Mavericks in December 1996. He returned to the team in February 2008.

improved by 23 wins. Kidd led the league in triple-doubles. Jackson and Mashburn both averaged more than 24 points per game.

The trio didn't last long, however. Mashburn missed most of the next season with injuries. Jackson and Kidd did not get along. By the middle of the 1996–97 season, none of the three played for Dallas anymore.

Kidd was dealt to the Phoenix Suns in December 1996. Mashburn was traded to the Miami Heat two months later. Three days after Mashburn moved on, Jackson was shipped to the New Jersey Nets. The book was closed on the Three J's. In 2008 the New Jersey Nets traded Kidd back to the Mavericks during the middle of the season. He was 34 years old but still an effective player. Kidd spent four more seasons in Dallas and was a key part of the veteran squad that finally lifted a championship trophy in 2011. He played 19 years in the NBA and retired as one of the best point guards of all time.

BUILDING A CHAMPION

Dallas made the playoffs in 1990 but missed out for the rest of the decade. Despite that, a new group of stars started shining in the late 1990s. Small forward Michael Finley was the key piece coming back to Dallas in the Jason Kidd trade. Finley was not only a solid scorer but also a durable player. He led the NBA in minutes played three times while

Mark Cuban

Billionaire entrepreneur Mark Cuban bought the Mavericks in 2000. He became one of the most visible and outspoken owners in the NBA. Cuban was a passionate fan. At times his passion crossed the line. Cuban often criticized officials. He once ran onto the court during a game in 2009 to yell at an opposing player. For that he was fined $25,000 by the league. It was just one of his many fines. By 2020 Cuban had reportedly been fined more than $3 million by the NBA.

Point guard Steve Nash (13) and forwards Dirk Nowitzki (41) and Michael Finley (4) led Dallas to the Western Conference finals in 2003.

with the Mavericks. And he did it while playing a fast-paced style under head coach Don Nelson.

Running that fast break in the early 2000s was point guard Steve Nash. Like Finley, Nash started his career in Phoenix. But he struggled in his first few seasons. After coming to Dallas in a trade, he grew into an All-Star. Nash was an intelligent player and an extremely creative passer. He excelled at finding Finley and Nowitzki for open shots. Led by this Big Three, Dallas went all the way to the Western Conference finals in 2002–03.

Nash eventually left Dallas to go back to Phoenix after the 2003–04 season. The Mavericks could not afford him anymore. A big reason was that Nowitzki had become such a big star. The German power forward had needed time to adjust to the NBA after he was drafted in 1998. He struggled through his rookie year, averaging fewer than nine points per game. Even he wondered if he could succeed in the best league in the world.

However, the next season his scoring doubled. From that point on, he was one of the best players in the NBA. The 7-foot Nowitzki had the size of a center but the skills of a guard. He was one of the best three-point shooters in the league for much of his career. His combination of inside and outside skills made him one of the toughest players to guard. And Nowitzki became a pioneer for European NBA stars. In 2007 Nowitzki became the first European to win the NBA MVP Award.

Nowitzki's rise took Dallas to new heights. He led the Mavericks to the NBA Finals for the first time in 2006. Five years later, he was the Finals MVP when Dallas captured its first title. It was the crowning achievement of a career that lasted 21 seasons. When Nowitzki finally retired in 2019, he had played his entire career in Dallas. He had been the franchise's all-time leading scorer for 11 years.

While Nowitzki was the key player, Dallas's 2010–11 title-winning team was filled with solid veterans. Shooting guard Jason Terry was the team's other key scorer. The 33-year-old was at his best coming off the bench. He had already won the NBA's Sixth Man of the Year award two seasons earlier. He proved it again when he scored a game-high 27

Mavericks center Tyson Chandler drives to the basket during the 2011 NBA Finals.

points off the bench in the clinching Game 6 of the NBA Finals against Miami.

Anchoring the defense was center Tyson Chandler. He came over in a trade with the Charlotte Bobcats and led Dallas in rebounding in 2010–11. The team also had tough guards. In addition to the veteran Kidd, 26-year-old J. J. Barea stepped up in the playoffs. He actually started more postseason games (three) than regular-season contests (two). He was in the starting lineup for Game 6 and added 15 points.

THE MODERN MAVERICKS

Dallas struggled to stay on top after winning the NBA Finals in 2011. Coach Rick Carlisle kept the team in the playoff hunt most years, but Dallas eventually faded out of the playoff picture by 2016–17. By the 2018 draft, the Mavericks were back on the rise.

Luka Dončić averaged 21.2 points, 7.8 rebounds, and 6.0 assists in 2018–19 and was named that season's Rookie of the Year.

Mavericks fans saw a lot of Dirk Nowitzki in their new star, guard Luka Dončić. Like Nowitzki, Dončić was from Europe. He grew up in Slovenia. He was another player who could do everything. On February 28, 2020, Dončić turned 21 years old. Five days later, he broke Kidd's record for triple-doubles by a Dallas Maverick. It was his twenty-second triple-double in only 122 career games. That year he also made his first All-Star team.

In 2021–22 Kidd returned to the Mavericks as head coach. He and Dončić led Dallas to the Western Conference finals. With one of the league's best players on the floor every night, the Mavericks were set up for a bright future.

CHAPTER FOUR

MAVERICK MOMENTS

The Mavericks made their first deep playoff run in 1987–88. After defeating the Houston Rockets and Denver Nuggets in the first two rounds of the 1988 postseason, Dallas matched up with the Los Angeles Lakers.

Los Angeles was the defending NBA champion. Its roster featured two of the greatest players ever, point guard Earvin "Magic" Johnson and center Kareem Abdul-Jabbar. The team had a third future Hall of Famer in forward James Worthy. Additionally, the Lakers' Pat Riley was regarded as one of the league's top coaches.

With their stacked roster, the Lakers were heavy favorites against the Mavericks. But Dallas did not fold. The Mavericks battled back after losing the first two games in Los Angeles. They won Games 3 and 4 at home by double-digit margins.

Forward Sam Perkins (41) was one of six Dallas players who averaged at least 10 points per game during the Mavericks' run to the Western Conference finals in 1988.

The Lakers recovered to win Game 5, putting the Mavericks in a must-win situation in Game 6.

After a tight game, the Mavericks were clinging to a 104–102 lead with 11 seconds left. Los Angeles had the ball. After several passes, the Lakers found an open Worthy on the baseline. However, Dallas forward Sam Perkins came over to challenge his layup. He forced Worthy to miss the shot. Mavericks center James Donaldson was fouled after grabbing the rebound with two seconds left.

Donaldson then made one of his foul shots. Dallas fouled Johnson before he could ever attempt a game-tying three-point shot. Johnson hit one free throw, but Dallas hung on for a 105–103 win. When the final buzzer sounded, Rolando Blackman spiked the ball on the court. It was the biggest win in Mavericks franchise history up to that point.

GETTING OVER THE HUMP

Guards Steve Nash and Michael Finley had helped turn the Mavericks back into contenders during the early 2000s. By the 2005–06 season, both had left as free agents. Of the original Big Three, Dirk Nowitzki was the lone star remaining in Dallas. However, Nowitzki quickly proved that he was capable of carrying the team.

The Mavericks' opponent in the Western Conference finals was the Phoenix Suns. Nash was not only the Suns' point guard.

He was also the league's MVP that season.

Dallas and Phoenix split the first four games, making Game 5 a crucial contest. Nowitzki set the tone early, making two three-pointers and throwing down a thunderous dunk in the first quarter. He scored 13 points in the opening period and added four points in the second. The Mavs led 58–55 at halftime.

Dirk Nowitzki attempts a layup against the Phoenix Suns during the 2006 Western Conference finals.

In the third quarter, Nowitzki scored 11 more points, including a three-pointer that gave Dallas the lead at 80–77. Then, in the fourth quarter, Nowitzki caught fire. In one of the most iconic performances of his career, Nowitzki scored 22 points in the final period. He capped it off with a three-pointer with less than two minutes left. The shot gave him a franchise playoff record 50 points. The Mavericks won the game 117–101.

Two days later, Dallas defeated Phoenix in Game 6 to win the series. For the first time in their 26-year history, the Mavericks were in the NBA Finals.

CHAMPIONS AT LAST!

The 2011 NBA Finals featured a rematch of the 2006 Finals between the Mavericks and the Miami Heat. Following Dallas's epic comeback in Game 2, the series was tied at one game apiece. The series then shifted to Dallas, where the Mavs lost Game 3 by two points before recovering to win Games 4 and 5.

Game 6 was back in Miami. LeBron James made his first four shots as the Heat led 20–11 early in the game. However, Nowitzki, Jason Terry, and J. J. Barea helped put the Mavericks in control.

Late in the second quarter, Terry scored 10 straight Dallas points to help his team take the lead at halftime. Nowitzki began the third quarter with a jump shot to put the Mavericks up 55–51. The Heat answered with five straight points to take the lead, but Barea's layup gave Dallas the lead for good.

Nowitzki scored eight points in the third quarter and 10 more in the fourth to secure the championship. After shooting 1-for-12 for three points in the first half, Nowitzki hit eight of his 15 shots in the second half, scoring 18 points. He was named

International Icon

On November 11, 2014, Dirk Nowitzki became the ninth-leading scorer in NBA history, surpassing Houston Rockets legend Hakeem Olajuwon. By passing Olajuwon, the German-born Nowitzki also became the top foreign-born scorer in NBA history.

Dirk Nowitzki, *left*, holds up the NBA Finals MVP Award while Jason Kidd poses with the NBA Championship trophy after the Mavericks' 2011 Finals win.

NBA Finals MVP, and, for the first time ever, the Mavericks were the champions.

"This team has so much heart, so much determination," owner Mark Cuban said following the team's long-awaited championship. "I love every one of them."

LUKA'S NIGHT

By the time Nowitzki retired in 2019, Dallas had a new star in Luka Dončić.

In his first NBA seasons, Dončić developed a reputation as one of the league's most clutch players. A marathon game during the 2020 playoffs helped cement that legend.

The Mavericks weren't sure Dončić would even play Game 4 of the 2020 opening round against the Los Angeles Clippers. The guard was injured with a sore ankle. But Dončić suited up and then took apart Los Angeles.

Dončić finished the game with a triple-double of 43 points, 17 rebounds, and 13 assists. His efforts helped Dallas overcome a 21-point second-quarter hole. But the Clippers hung tough. The game went into overtime tied 121–121. With 50 seconds left in the extra session, Dončić tied the game 130–130 with a crafty runner. His spinning layup with 19 seconds remaining put Dallas in front. Los Angeles responded with a three-pointer from forward Marcus Morris.

Special Company

Only two players in NBA history have scored at least 40 points in a playoff game, capped by a buzzer-beater while their team was trailing. One was Luka Dončić in 2020. The other was Chicago Bulls legend Michael Jordan in 1989.

Teammates mob Luka Dončić (77) after his game-winning shot beat the Los Angeles Clippers in Game 4 of the 2020 Western Conference playoffs opening round.

Dallas had one last chance to win it. The Mavericks went to their 21-year-old star.

Dončić caught the inbounds pass with 3.7 seconds left. He used a crossover dribble to gain some separation against the defender. Then, from the left wing, Dončić hoisted a three-pointer from several feet behind the arc. When it went through the hoop, the Mavericks rushed to Dončić in celebration.

"Bang! Bang! It's good!" exclaimed TV broadcaster Mike Breen. "Dončić wins the game at the buzzer!"

Dončić was the youngest player ever to hit a buzzer-beater in an NBA playoff game. Breen added moments later: "We are witnessing the next great star in the NBA."

As they looked to the future, Mavericks fans hoped so as well.

TIMELINE

1980

The Mavericks join the NBA as an expansion franchise.

1981

Dallas drafts Mark Aguirre, Rolando Blackman, and Jay Vincent.

1984

The Mavericks defeat the Seattle SuperSonics in five games to win the first playoff series in team history.

1987

The Mavericks finish 55–27 to win the Midwest Division, the first division title in franchise history.

1988

The Mavericks reach the Western Conference finals for the first time, falling to the Los Angeles Lakers in a seven-game series.

1993

Dallas completes an 11–71 season, the second-worst record in NBA history.

1994

The Mavericks finish 13–69, posting the NBA's worst record for the second-straight season.

1998

In a series of draft-day trades, Dallas acquires rookie forward Dirk Nowitzki and young point guard Steve Nash.

2000

Mark Cuban buys a majority stake in the Mavericks for $280 million.

2001

The Mavericks begin playing at the American Airlines Center.

2006

The Mavericks advance to the NBA Finals for the first time, losing to the Miami Heat in six games.

2007

The Mavericks complete a 67–15 season, the best record in franchise history, before losing to the Golden State Warriors in the first round of the playoffs.

2011

The Mavericks defeat the Miami Heat 4–2 to win their first NBA championship.

2017

The Mavericks end the season 33–49 and finish in last place in their division for the first time since 1993–94.

2018

Dallas acquires rookie Luka Dončić in a draft-day trade with the Atlanta Hawks.

2019

Mavs star Dirk Nowitzki retires after 21 seasons with a single franchise, an NBA record.

2021

Dallas hires former Mavericks guard Jason Kidd as head coach. In his first season, the Mavericks finish 52–30 and reach the Western Conference finals.

FACTS

FRANCHISE HISTORY
Dallas Mavericks (1980–)

NBA CHAMPIONSHIPS
2011

KEY PLAYERS
Mark Aguirre (1981–89)
Rolando Blackman (1981–92)
Brad Davis (1980–92)
Luka Dončić (2018–)
Michael Finley (1996–2005)
Derek Harper (1983–94,
  1996–97)
Jason Kidd (1994–96, 2008–12)
Steve Nash (1998–2004)
Dirk Nowitzki (1998–2019)
Jason Terry (2004–12)

KEY COACHES
Rick Carlisle (2008–21)
Dick Motta (1980–87, 1994–96)
Don Nelson (1997–2005)

HOME ARENAS
Reunion Arena (1980–2001)
American Airlines Center
  (2001–)

TEAM
TRIVIA

MAVERICK OWNER

The Mavericks' nickname was inspired by the TV show *Maverick*, which aired from 1957 to 1962. The show's star, James Garner, was one of the team's original owners.

GROUNDBREAKER

In 2001 Mavericks center Wang Zhizhi became the first Chinese player to play in the NBA. He played in 60 games for Dallas over parts of two seasons, averaging 5.5 points and 2.0 rebounds per game.

SOLD OUT!

The Mavericks sold out every home game (regular season and playoffs) from December 15, 2001, until crowds were reduced across the league due to the COVID-19 pandemic in 2020.

HONORING A LEGEND

Following the death of Los Angeles Lakers legend Kobe Bryant in 2020, the Mavericks announced that they would retire No. 24 in Bryant's honor. They were the only NBA team, other than the Lakers, to retire his jersey.

GLOSSARY

assist
A pass that leads directly to a basket.

draft
A system that allows teams to acquire new players coming into a league.

franchise
A sports organization, including the top-level team and all minor league affiliates.

free agent
A player whose rights are not owned by any team.

general manager
An executive who runs a team and is responsible for finding and signing players.

prime
The age range in which an athlete is able to perform at the peak of his or her abilities.

rebound
To catch the ball after a shot has been missed.

retire
To end one's career.

rookie
A professional athlete in his or her first year of competition.

superstar
A player who is extremely talented, has great public appeal, and can often command a high salary.

triple-double
Accumulating 10 or more of three certain statistics in a game.

veteran
A player who has played for many years.

MORE
INFORMATION

BOOKS

Flynn, Brendan. *The NBA Encyclopedia for Kids.* Minneapolis, MN: Abdo Publishing, 2022.

Mahoney, Brian. *GOATs of Basketball.* Minneapolis, MN: Abdo Publishing, 2022.

Ybarra, Andres. *Great Basketball Debates.* Minneapolis, MN: Abdo Publishing, 2019.

ONLINE RESOURCES

Booklinks
NONFICTION NETWORK
FREE! ONLINE NONFICTION RESOURCES

To learn more about the Dallas Mavericks, please visit **abdobooklinks.com** or scan this QR code. These links are routinely monitored and updated to provide the most current information available.

INDEX

ABOUT THE AUTHOR

Drew Silverman is a freelance sportswriter based in Philadelphia, Pennsylvania. He graduated from Syracuse University and has worked for ESPN, Comcast SportsNet, and NBC Sports. He also was sports editor of the Bulletin, a newspaper in Philadelphia. He lives in Philadelphia with his wife, Sara; his son, Charlie; and his daughter, Emma.

South Huntington

JAN 09 2023

3499